INTRODUCING

Keynesian Economics

Peter Pugh and Chris Garratt

Edited by Richard Appignanesi

ICON BOOKS UK   TOTEM BOOKS USA

This edition published in the UK
in 2000 by Icon Books Ltd.,
Grange Road, Duxford,
Cambridge CB2 4QF
email: info@iconbooks.co.uk
www.iconbooks.co.uk

Distributed in the UK, Europe,
Canada, South Africa and Asia by the
Penguin Group: Penguin Books Ltd.,
27 Wrights Lane, London W8 5TZ

This edition published in Australia
in 2000 by Allen & Unwin Pty. Ltd.,
PO Box 8500, 9 Atchison Street,
St. Leonards NSW 2065

Previously published in the UK and
Australia in 1993 under the title
Keynes for Beginners

Reprinted 1995, 1997

This edition published in the United
States in 2000 by Totem Books
Inquiries to: PO Box 223,
Canal Street Station,
New York, NY 10013

In the United States,
distributed to the trade by
National Book Network Inc.,
4720 Boston Way, Lanham,
Maryland 20706

Previously published in the
United States in 1994 under the
title *Introducing Keynes*

Library of Congress catalog
card number applied for

ISBN 1 84046 157 8

Printed and bound in Australia
by McPherson's Printing Group, Victoria

John Maynard Keynes (1883-1946)

John Maynard Keynes was the greatest and certainly the most influential economist of the 20th century. Keynes' economic theories sprang from direct practical experience of three key moments of the 20th century: **the post-World War One peace settlement, the Great Depression** and **World War Two.**

The Keynes Family Background

John Maynard Keynes was born on 5 June 1883 at 6, Harvey Road, Cambridge, a house built by his parents and occupied by them from 1882 until after Maynard's death. His mother, Florence, born in1861, lived there with the same solid furnishings and William Morris wallpaper till she died in 1958.

Pioneers of Youth Culture

Leonard Woolf (1880-1969), one of its leading lights, encapsulated Bloomsbury's attitude exactly:

WE WERE CONVINCED THAT EVERYONE OVER 25, WITH PERHAPS ONE OR TWO REMARKABLE EXCEPTIONS, WAS 'HOPELESS,' HAVING LOST THE ÉLAN OF YOUTH, THE CAPACITY TO FEEL AND THE ABILITY TO DISTINGUISH TRUTH FROM FALSEHOOD...

...WE FOUND OURSELVES LIVING IN THE SPRINGTIME OF CONSCIOUS REVOLT AGAINST THE SOCIAL, POLITICAL, RELIGIOUS, MORAL, INTELLECTUAL AND ARTISTIC INSTITUTIONS, BELIEFS AND STANDARDS OF OUR FATHERS AND GRANDFATHERS...

...WE WERE OUT TO CONSTRUCT SOME--THING NEW; WE WERE IN THE VAN OF THE BUILDERS OF A NEW SOCIETY WHICH SHOULD BE FREE, RATIONAL, CIVILIZED, PURSUING TRUTH AND BEAUTY. Ω

NEVER TRUST ANYONE OVER 25 30 35 40

BORN

The word *Bloomsbury* was to pass into the English language as a cultural phenomenon rather than a geographical area. Keynes entered this way of life with enthusiasm and supported some of the poorer members financially. His great love affair of the time was with the artist **Duncan Grant (1885-1978)**, a cousin of **Lytton Strachey (1880-1932)**.

Keynes, always keen on statistics, whether on the economy, cricket or golf, kept full details of his sexual encounters both with Grant and others, entering them in his diary. At a time when any homosexual act was a criminal offence, Keynes identified them with initials, nicknames or simply descriptions.

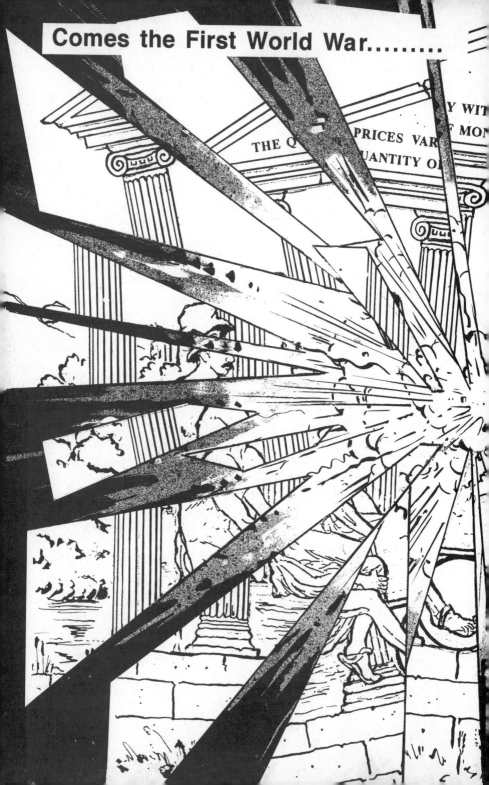

Comes the First World War.........

With the outbreak of War in 1914, Keynes moved into the Treasury and was soon advising at the highest level. It could be argued that he was instrumental in bringing the Americans into the War...

...BY PERSUADING THE BRITISH GOVERNMENT TO MAINTAIN CONVERTIBILITY IN EARLY 1917...,

...AND THAT'S GOOD FOR US, SINCE WE'VE GOT MOST OF THE WORLD'S GOLD!

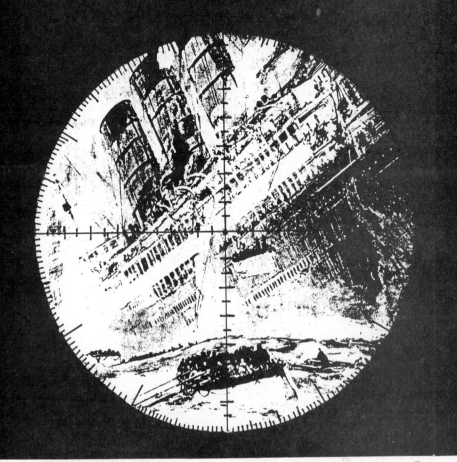

The Germans increased their submarine activity, a key factor in persuading the Americans to declare War. Keynes was promoted to head a new department to deal with all the questions of external finance.

VERSAILLES TREATY SIGNED!

In 1919, at the Paris Peace Conference in Versailles, Keynes was in charge of financial matters and for two months had been preparing the Treasury position on the level of German indemnity payments.

GERMANY TO PAY £24 BILLION REPARATIONS!

The War Cabinet appointed a committee, largely under the influence of the Bank of England, which recommended a figure of **£24 billion** (£1000 billion in today's terms).

Keynes' team produced two figures -

The Allies, who had lent money to many European countries but had borrowed from the USA, were worried that they might be left with bad debts in Europe and firm commitments to the US. Keynes devised "a grand scheme for the rehabilitation of Europe", which entailed a scaling down of Britain's demands on Germany, in return for a remission of some of its debt to the US.

All inter-Ally debts would be reduced and European credit would be revised. The US would be assured of demand for its exports and the Central Powers - the former enemy - would obtain funds to feed their people.

U.S. SAYS: THANKS - BUT NO THANKS!

The U.S. did not buy Keynes' proposition.

Keynes resigned his position at the Treasury to write *The Economic Consequences of the Peace*, one of the most important and influential books of the 20th century.

The Economic Consequences of the Peace

In it, Keynes attacked the three main leaders of the Allies

The Remarkable Foresight of J.M. Keynes

He wrote:

"I am utterly worn out mentally and nervously and deeply disgusted, depressed and dismayed at the unjust and unwise proposals we have made to Germany."

How did Keynes measure Germany's capacity to pay reparations?

"Her only means of paying was through an export surplus. Pre-War her deficit had been £74 million. By reducing imports and increasing exports, she might turn this into a £50 million surplus. Spread over 30 years this would come to a capital sum of £1700 million invested at 6%. Add £100-200 million for transfers of gold, property etc. and £2 billion is a safe maximum figure of Germany's capacity to pay."

Apart from her capacity to pay, Keynes doubted Germany's **willingness.**

"I do not believe that any of these tributes will continue to be paid, at the best, for more than a very few years. They do not square with human nature or agree with the spirit of the age."

37

He put forward the alternative.

GERMAN DAMAGES LIMITED TO £2000 MILLION

CANCEL INTER-ALLY DEBTS

CREATION OF EUROPEAN FREE TRADE AREA.

International Loan to Stabilize Exchanges.

Encouragement of Germany's natural organizing role in Eastern Europe, including Russia.

And if Keynes' measures were not adopted, what then?

"Vengeance, I dare predict, will not be limp. Nothing can delay for long that final civil war between the forces of reaction and the despairing convulsions of revolution, before which the horrors of the late German war will fade into nothing and will destroy, whoever is the victor, the civilization and progress of our generation."

John Maynard Keynes.

Keynes' book became world-famous, bringing praise from all sides.

Arthur Pigou (1877-1959), who succeeded Marshall as Professor of Political Economy at Cambridge, spoke for the economic establishment.

Others have since argued that its influence damaged world affairs, for 3 reasons:

41

For Keynes' biographer, **Robert Skidelsky (b.1939)**,

IT MARKED A RADICAL SHIFT IN KEYNES' THOUGHT FROM THE 19th CENTURY ASSUMPTION OF AUTOMATIC ECONOMIC PROGRESS SUSTAINED BY LIBERAL INSTITUTIONS TO A VIEW OF THE FUTURE IN WHICH PROSPERITY WOULD HAVE TO BE STRENUOUSLY WON IN THE TEETH OF THE ADVERSE CIRCUMSTANCES WHICH THE WAR HAD CREATED.

After the War, Keynes returned to Cambridge where he taught, lectured and wrote. From 1922, he lectured on the *Theory of Money* before changing, in 1932, to the *Monetary Theory of Production.* He continued his association with Bloomsbury which remained a strong influence culturally, if not in any other sense.

BLOOMSBURY WAS THE CONDUIT FOR SUCH INTELLECTUAL GIANTS AS DOSTOEVSKY, PROUST, CHEKHOV, CEZANNE, MATISSE, PICASSO AND FREUD.

Keynes supplemented his income through journalism, writing for *The Sunday Times*, the *Manchester Guardian*, the *Evening Standard* and *The Nation* (later absorbed by the *New Statesman)*, and the American magazines *Everybody's* and *New Republic*.

THE TIMES – WEATHERCOCK OF THE BRITISH ESTABLISHMENT – REMAINED HOSTILE FOLLOWING MY CRITICISMS OF THE VERSAILLES 'PEACEMAKERS'.

He also indulged in currency speculation. Although nearly cleaned out in 1920, he bounced back to make steady profits throughout the decade.

THUD!

Keynes Marries a Russian Ballerina

He abandoned his homosexual affairs when he met and fell in love with the Russian dancer, **Lydia Lopokova (1892-1981).** They were married in 1925. It had *not* been love at first sight......

But when they met, Keynes was overcome by her charm. There were no children from their marriage, but Lydia was a great source of joy to Keynes for the rest of his life.

Having received little formal education, Lydia was nevertheless a highly intelligent, free spirit. Her English could be idiosyncratic, described by Keynes as *"Lydiaspeak"*.

45

Lydia was not accepted by all of Keynes' friends. Leonard and Virginia Woolf were highly critical of her, as indeed they were of Keynes, who, they thought, had a brilliant mind but a poor character.

It was probably for Lydia that Keynes provided the funds to build the Cambridge Arts Theatre in the 1930s.

The need for a theatre was pressing because the town's two commercial theatres had closed. The New Theatre had become a cinema and the Festival Theatre, which had enjoyed a reputation beyond Cambridge in the late 1920s and early 1930s, had run out of wealthy backers. Furthermore, the ADC suffered a fire and lost its stage in November 1933.

The new Arts Theatre, financed by Keynes, opened on February 3rd 1936, the eve of publication of the *General Theory,* with a programme featuring the Vic-Wells Ballet.

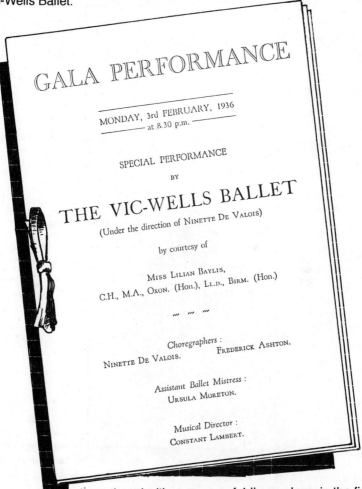

GALA PERFORMANCE

MONDAY, 3rd FEBRUARY, 1936
at 8.30 p.m.

SPECIAL PERFORMANCE

BY

THE VIC-WELLS BALLET

(Under the direction of NINETTE DE VALOIS)

by courtesy of

MISS LILIAN BAYLIS,
C.H., M.A., OXON. (Hon.), LL.D., BIRM. (Hon.)

''' ''' '''

Choreographers :
NINETTE DE VALOIS.   FREDERICK ASHTON.

Assistant Ballet Mistress :
URSULA MORETON.

Musical Director :
CONSTANT LAMBERT.

It continued with a season of 4 Ibsen plays, in the first and last of which Lydia took the female leads. In 1938, Keynes transformed the theatre into a trust and it has continued to operate successfully ever since.

Return to the Gold Standard

Keynes spent much of the 1920s arguing against Britain's return to the Gold Standard at sterling's pre-War dollar parity of $4.86. In 1923 he published *A Tract on Monetary Reform*, arguing that Britain should not go back to the pre-War Gold Standard system.

Its central theme is that monetary policy should be used to stabilize the price level and also the demand for money. By varying the amount of credit available to business, the fluctuations in the business cycle could be ironed out.

A Preview of the Exchange Rate Mechanism?

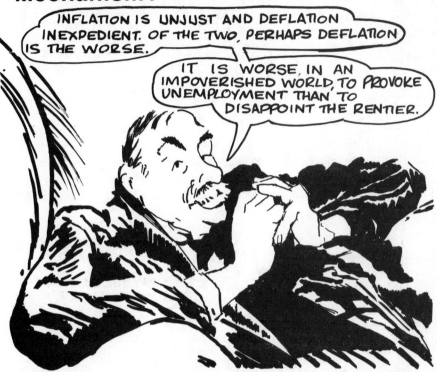

In Keynes' view, the management of domestic prices in the interests of business and social stability would be impossible if Britain returned to the Gold Standard at the pre-War parity. Faced with a choice, price stability was more important than **exchange rate stability.**

THE CONTRACTS AND BUSINESS EXPECTATIONS WHICH ASSUME A STABLE EXCHANGE MUST BE FAR FEWER, EVEN IN A TRADING COUNTRY SUCH AS ENGLAND, THAN THOSE WHICH PRESUME A STABLE LEVEL OF INTERNAL PRICES.

Exchange rate policy should be subordinated to the needs of the domestic economy. As most of the world's gold was in the US, a return to the Gold Standard would sacrifice the economic control to the federal Reserve Board of the US.

THE U.S. FEDERAL RESERVE BOARD IN THOSE DAYS... AND TODAY THE GERMAN BUNDESBANK?

Britain's economy on fast track to recovery in 1992.

Contrary to the classical view, Keynes felt that economic health was too important to be left to a **laissez-faire** approach - or to 'market forces'.

ECONOMIC MANAGEMENT MUST BE PART OF GOVERNMENT!

OH?

Keynes was opposed by all the pillars of the economic establishment.

As for financial journalists, Keynes wrote to *The Times* on March 28th 1925:

> To debate monetary reform with a City editor is like debating Darwinism with a bishop 60 years ago. But even bishops - so why not City editors? - move in the end.
>
> Yours Faithfully,
> JOHN MAYNARD KEYNES,
> Kings College,
> Cambridge.

He wrote to Lydia:

No! The economist is not king; quite true. But he ought to be! He is a better and wiser governor than the general or the diplomatist or the oratorial lawyer. In the modern, over-populated world, which can only live at all by nice adjustments, he is not only useful but necessary.

Must stop now and catch the post.

love Maynard X.

Keynes lost and in 1925, with Winston Churchill as Chancellor of the Exchequer, Britain returned to the Gold Standard with the pound fixed at its pre-War parity of $4.86. This prompted Keynes to write *The Economic Consequences of Mr.Churchill.*

The policy of improving the exchange by 10% involves a reduction of 10% in the sterling receipts of our export industries. The policy of reducing credit would only reduce wages and the cost of living by creating unemployment. Deflation does not reduce wages automatically. **It reduces them by causing unemployment**.

Whatever the argument for a return to the Gold Standard, mainly that the 19th century had been a long period of economic stabiltiy and steady growth, history is on Keynes' side. Virtually everyone is now agreed that the pound was overvalued between 1925 and 1931.

BLACK WEDNESDAY!

JUST AS THE POUND WAS OVERVALUED WHEN WE CAME OUT OF THE E.R.M. IN 1992.

When at last Britain came off the Gold Standard in 1931, Keynes wrote:

By the return to the gold standard in 1925, at an unsuitable parity, the bank had set itself a problem of adjustments so difficult as to have been well-nigh impossible. On the one hand it was obviously impractical to enforce, by high bank rate or by the contraction of credit, a deflation sufficiently drastic to bring about a reduction in internal costs appropriate to the parity adopted. On the other hand the maintenance of a low bank rate which would have rendered London unattractive to foreign short-term funds would have led to a rapid loss of gold by the Bank and a much earlier collapse of the Gold Standard.

TAP-TAP-TAP-TAP-TAP-TAP-TAP-TAP-RING!

The actual course adopted by the bank was a middle way, and as a result, the insecure structure collapsed.

TOO LATE ANYWAY —
—WE'RE RIGHT IN THE MIDDLE OF THE GREAT DEPRESSION!

Some prices, such as those determined internationally, rose rapidly, others less so. Wages adjusted even more slowly. The worst affected were those companies deeply involved in the export trade and a massive trade deficit was only averted by keeping the general economy depressed. Keynes criticised the policy of the Bank of England and its restriction of credit.

The policy can only attain its end by intensifying unemployment without limit, until the workers are ready to accept the necessary reduction of money wages under the pressure of hard facts.....deflation does not reduce wages automatically. It reduces them by causing unemployment. The proper object of dear money is to check an incipient boom. *Woe to those who use it to aggravate a depression!*

NOT MY WORDS, —BUT THOSE OF J.M.KEYNES!

Margaret Thatcher

Full Steam Ahead - to the Crash!

While Britain struggled with high unemployment throughout the 1920s, the US prospered. Unemployment was very low and production, wages and profits rose steadily, year after year. Prices remained stable and economists and politicians felt that the country was not just experiencing the upswing of the normal trade cycle, because this should have brought rising prices.

This belief led to some euphoria. If profits were to rise forever they had better get their hands

WE'VE FOUND THE SECRET OF PERMANENT ECONOMIC STABILITY!

on the shares of those companies benefiting from this "permanent" rise in profits. Share prices rose to ridiculous levels.

57

The Wall Street Crash - and World Depression

The Crash came in October 1929, and within a month,

shares had fallen by

a third.

They paused and even rose slightly in April 1930.
This was a dead cat bounce; they then plunged again

and carried on

falling

for another

2

years.

By the middle of 1932, the average industrial share was about 15% of its price in October 1929. If the Wall Street Crash ushered in the World Slump of the early 1930s, it wasn't the real cause.

The real cause was the good, old fashioned

Upswing - Downswing of the trade cycle.

The upswing in the 1920s had been really strong.

THE OUTPUT OF
CAPITAL GOODS ROSE
BY NEARLY A QUARTER
BETWEEN 1927 AND
1929...

The downswing, which actually began *before* the Wall Street Crash, was going to be strong too.

...BY 1932, THE OUTPUT OF
CAPITAL GOODS WAS ONLY A
QUARTER OF THE LEVEL OF 1929...

The fall in the output of consumer goods, though less severe, was also strong, and as a result industrial production in 1932 was only half what it had been in 1929.

... UNEMPLOYMENT IN THE
U.S. ROSE FROM 1½ MILLION
IN 1929 TO **12 MILLION**
IN 1932.

The Effect on Germany

The repercussions were felt throughout the world, because of the precarious nature of international debt. The US had invested heavily overseas in the 1920s, especially in Germany. Towards the end of the 1920s, US investment in Germany declined.....

.......German industry, starved of funds, began to contract and Germany could not meet reparation and other debt repayments to France and Britain. This led to the same scramble for cash that had accompanied the Wall Street Crash. The spiral worsened............

The Fall and Rise of John Maynard Keynes

As in the 1920s' slump, Keynes was again almost wiped out personally.

However, he survived, and by 1936 he had rebuilt his fortune to £500,000 (probably £25 million in 2000 terms).

Most of his gains were made in the US, where Wall Street tripled from its low point in 1932, while London stocks hardly appreciated. This was interesting, in view of the fact that Keynes publicly disagreed with his closest City associate, **Oswald Falk (1881-1972),** following Falk's memorandum in 1930.

MEMORANDUM

Date: April 1930

From: Oswald Falk

To: British investors
Stockbrokers
Financial Advisers
Anyone with a bit of Spare Cash

British Industry is finished.

Investors should sell their British securities and buy U.S. ones.

Yrs, Oswald X.

The General Theory, 1936

The world depression provided the background for Keynes' seminal work, *The General Theory of Employment, Interest and Money,* published in 1936. If *The Economic Consequences of the Peace* was one of the most influential books of the 20th century, *The General Theory* is probably <u>the</u> most influential.

IT'S NOT EASY READING!

PUBLIC READING ROOM
NO SNORING

Paul Samuelson (b.1915), economist and Keynes disciple

"It is a badly written book, poorly organized...it is arrogant, bad-tempered, polemical........it abounds in mare's nests and confusions: involuntary unemployment, wage units, the equality of savings and investments, the timing of the multiplier, interactions of marginal efficiency upon the rate of interest and many others.......flashes of insight and intuition intersperse tedious algebra. An awkward definition suddenly gives way to unforgettable cadenza. When it is finally mastered, we find its analysis to be obvious and at the same time new. In short, it is a work of genius."

Long before 1936, Keynes was a world-renowned figure, ensuring that anything he wrote would be instantly absorbed by anyone influential in the world of finance and economics throughout the world. On both sides of the Atlantic, it was the young economists who took to the book most fervently.

Keynes -The 'Einstein of Economics'

One of the sharpest critics of *The General Theory* was **Arthur Pigou (1877-1959)**. A pioneer of welfare economics, he had himself produced a general economic theory of government intervention. He saw *The General Theory* as a criticism of Marshall and of his own *Theory of Unemployment* (1933).

"Einstein actually did for Physics what Mr. Keynes believes himself to have done for Economics. Einstein developed a far-reaching generalization under which Newton's result can be subsumed as a special case. But he did not, in announcing his discovery, insinuate, through carefully barbed sentences, that Newton and those who had hitherto followed his lead were a gang of incompetent bunglers."

IF I'M THE "EINSTEIN", WHO WERE THE FORMER "NEWTONS" OF ECONOMICS?

In other words, what did Keynes revolutionize? Let's look at economics before Keynes.

Economics before Keynes

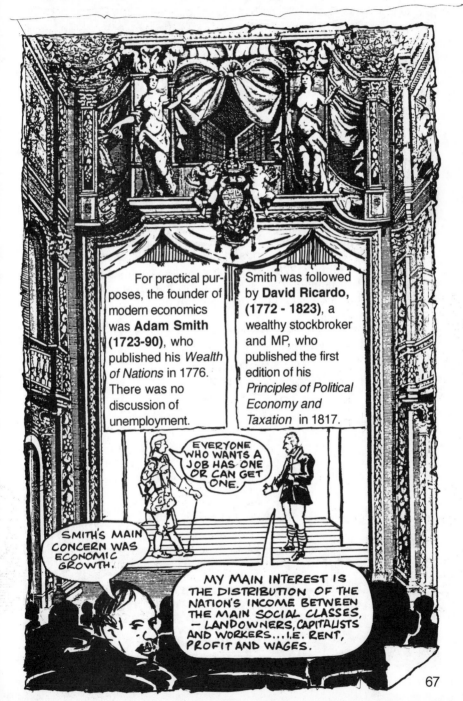

For practical purposes, the founder of modern economics was **Adam Smith (1723-90)**, who published his *Wealth of Nations* in 1776. There was no discussion of unemployment.

Smith was followed by **David Ricardo, (1772 - 1823)**, a wealthy stockbroker and MP, who published the first edition of his *Principles of Political Economy and Taxation* in 1817.

EVERYONE WHO WANTS A JOB HAS ONE OR CAN GET ONE.

SMITH'S MAIN CONCERN WAS ECONOMIC GROWTH.

MY MAIN INTEREST IS THE DISTRIBUTION OF THE NATION'S INCOME BETWEEN THE MAIN SOCIAL CLASSES. — LANDOWNERS, CAPITALISTS AND WORKERS...I.E. RENT, PROFIT AND WAGES.

Ricardo's Reply

It **is** possible to have a glut of commodities, but only a **temporary** glut of a **particular** commodity. Some sudden shock - a war, a change in taxation or of fashion - can bring a decline in demand and consequent unemployment for those producing the commodity. However, as demand for one commodity falls, demand for another will rise. Before long, equilibrium will have been re-established. The only unemployment, of men or machinery, that is possible is temporary unemployment.

Ricardo's reply to Malthus became the enduring thesis of orthodox economists from the 1820s to the 1920s.

Say's Law

To refute Malthus' view of the spectre of general unemployment, Ricardo invoked Say's Law. **J.B. Say (1776-1832)** was a French economist who in 1803 put forward the view that "supply creates its own demand."

IN OTHER WORDS, THE PROCESS OF PUTTING A COMMODITY ON THE MARKET **CREATES** THE INCOME WITH WHICH THAT COMMODITY CAN BE BOUGHT.

Exactly enough income is generated to enable a population to buy everything that is produced.

BY DEFINITION, A GLUT OF COMMODITIES IS IMPOSSIBLE.

They had to, since there was no Stock Exchange for the raising of capital and bank lending was undeveloped.

Marx on the Trade Cycle

After Ricardo came **Karl Marx (1818-83)** who took over much of Smith and Ricardo's thinking, but asked a different question.

BOOM

BUST

WHY IS THERE SO MUCH PERIODIC UNEMPLOYMENT?

HE SAW IT AS THE CONSEQUENCE OF THE TRADE CYCLE.

In Marx's view, the trade cycle of boom and bust would get larger and larger, until the whole capitalist system collapsed.

He also saw the economies being increasingly dominated by large monopolies which would invest only **part** of their profits.

Was Marx Right?

With the mass unemployment of the 1920s, Marx's predictions seemed to have come true. The revolution that he had predicted had also come about - though, contrary to his expectation, in Russia - and it was to Soviet communism that many of the most intelligent and thoughtful looked for a solution.

WHAT THIS INTELLIGENTSIA OVERLOOKS IS MARX'S FORMULA THAT THE WORKERS' STANDARD OF LIVING WILL REMAIN AT SUBSISTENCE LEVEL.

In reality, even in the slump year of 1930, the British working man was twice as well off as his grandfather in 1860. Nevertheless Marx made a valid point.....

SOCIETY'S CAPACITY TO PRODUCE WILL OUTSTRIP ITS CAPACITY TO CONSUME.

The Trade Cycle

The other major development in 19th century economic thinking was the acceptance of the **trade** or **business cycle.** The cycle was believed to last 8 to 10 years.

After 3 or 4 more years of decline, everything levels off and begins to rise, setting the whole cycle in motion again.

By the early years of the 20th century, a great deal of thought had been given to the trade cycle throughout the industrialized world and a consensus had been reached on what **caused** the turns in the cycle.

A Difference between Capital Goods and Consumer Goods

What caused the downturn was that industries making **capital** goods, i.e. machinery and equipment used in the processes of production, expanded faster than those making **consumer** goods, i.e. goods bought in shops. As a result, when full employment was reached, production was distorted, with too much labour and money tied up in the production of capital as opposed to consumer goods.

The Accelerator

Why did the upswing bring a greater expansion of capital goods industries? The answer was **The Accelerator.** A small change in the demand for consumer goods leads to a **greater** change in the demand for the capital goods required to <u>produce</u> those consumer goods.

Example

A firm produces 10,000 electric toasters and sells them at £10 each. This production requires £400,000 of machinery.

Each year, 10% of its plant becomes obsolete, so it must buy £40,000 of new plant.

This could continue in equilibrium for ever but in an upswing, the demand for its toasters might increase, say 10%, to 11,000 toasters.

It already takes £40 of machinery to produce each toaster (£400,000 divided by 10,000) and the firm must now install another £40,000 of plant to make the extra toasters.

In that year it must increase its investment from £40,000 to £80,000, an increase of **100%**, to cope with an increase in consumer demand of **10%.**

Recession

And of course the same **Accelerator Principle** applies in reverse. When consumer demand drops back, the capital goods manufacturers' need to buy new plant drops back, again by a much bigger percentage.

Between 1913 and 1920, wages had risen very sharply. In fact, they had trebled.

The severe recession which began in 1920 did bring, as theory and experience suggested, a sharp fall in both wages and prices, and both declined by about a third in the next three years. However, British exports were still not competitive at the pre-War parity of $4.86 that the government used to take Britain back on to the Gold Standard.

WAGES WILL HAVE TO FALL STILL FURTHER AND WE BELIEVE THEY'LL DO SO AUTOMATICALLY.

I DOUBT THEY WILL WITHOUT FURTHER SAVAGE DEFLATIONARY MEASURES!

With unemployment already over 10%, Keynes felt this was too high a price for returning to the Gold Standard.

The General Strike of 1926

Mine-owners especially disagreed with Keynes and, pressured by the overvaluation of sterling's effect on their export prices, attempted to reduce wages by 10-25%. This led to the **General Strike** in 1926.

But in most other industries, wages stayed at 1925 levels and British exports remained uncompetitive for the rest of the decade. Unemployment also remained high.

Winston Churchill defended the return to the Gold Standard.

Orthodox 1920s economists said...

By 1931, especially in view of the sharp deterioration in the world situation, something had to give. By the end of July, the Bank was losing gold at the rate of £15 million a week and Britain's reserves were down to £133 million.

A Committee on National Expenditure was set up under **Sir George May (1871-1946)** –

WE RECOMMEND INCREASES IN TAXATION AND *DRASTIC CUTS* IN EXPENDITURE, PARTICULARLY ON UNEMPLOYMENT BENEFITS.

THIS IS THE MOST FOOLISH DOCUMENT I HAVE EVER HAD THE MISFORTUNE TO READ!

COMMITTEE ON NATIONAL

This report spread alarm further and the outflow of gold increased. Eventually, with the remaining reserves of gold disappearing, the government suspended gold payments.

The immediate effect was a plunge in the value of sterling from $4.86 to $3.58, a devaluation of 26%. This initially made British exports more competitive but other countries also devalued, raising tariffs in a vain attempt to protect employment. The effect on world trade was catastrophic. It fell to a third of its 1929 level. Unemployment in Britain reached 22%. In Germany and the U.S. it was even higher.

In the 1990s, we again faced the twin evils of recession and unemployment … and there is still the threat of a trade war.

What's the answer?

The orthodox response from those steeped in 19th century economic thinking was that full employment was the normal state of affairs and, given time, would return.

Keynes' Solutions

So much for the orthodox view. In **The General Theory**, Keynes proposed something new and different. In January 1935, he wrote to **George Bernard Shaw (1856-1950)**:

...I believe myself to be writing a book on economic theory which will largely rationalise (not, I suppose at once but in the course of the next few years) the way the world thinks about economic problems....

Keynes rejected the classical Benthamite belief in the **laissez-faire** free market and minimal state intervention.

He realized that the classical remedies - "to do nothing and wait for full employment to return automatically" - would no longer suffice.

Times had changed from when the high savings of the wealthy in the 19th century had brought a high rate of investment, sustaining progress and raising living standards.

He was conscious of the importance of business confidence.

Is the answer full employment?

Keynes challenged the accepted doctrine that the norm was full employment. "Why should it be?", he asked. This startled the orthodox, but it also carried a strong implication - that if full employment was not automatic, governments were **obliged** to act to bring it about.

What determines the level of employment?

For Keynes, the **level of output** determines the **level of employment.**
This in turn is determined by the level of effective demand, or the level of
purchases of goods and services.

To Keynes it was more sensible to employ people to do something - anything - as long as they were paid, rather than have them stand idle and be paid little or nothing. As usual he expressed his views graphically:

LET ME PUT IT THIS WAY...

...IF THE **TREASURY** WERE TO FILL OLD BOTTLES WITH BANKNOTES...

...BURY THEM AT SUITABLE DEPTHS IN DISUSED COALMINES, WHICH ARE THEN FILLED UP TO THE TOP WITH TOWN RUBBISH...

GARBAGE DISPOSAL

DANGER DISUSED MINESHAFT

WHOOPEE!

...AND LEAVE TO PRIVATE ENTERPRISE TO DIG THE MONEY UP AGAIN, THERE NEED BE NO MORE UNEMPLOYMENT!

BUT IN PRACTICE, THINGS DIDN'T WORK OUT QUITE THAT WAY...

Government action was necessary, perhaps by reducing interest rates or through public investment programmes.
In conjunction with the effect of the **Multiplier**, such actions should bring back full employment.

What is the Multiplier?

The **Multiplier** is tied up with the individual's **marginal propensity to consume** (MPC), which is the fraction of an individual's *increase* in income spent on consumption.

Example

increase in income	= £1000
spending on consumption	= £ 800
MPC	= 800/1000 or 0.8
Marginal propensity to *save*	= 200/1000 or 0.2

The Multiplier Effect...

For Keynes, the size of the **marginal propensity to consume** (MPC) was the key to the size of the change in the National Income necessary to bring about the ideal equilibrium in which producers would *produce* what consumers wanted to *consume*.

........or the MPC chain......

So........

the final multiplier effect won't be £1000 but

£1000 + £800 + £640 + £512 +........

The final multiplier effect should be a factor of **5**.

BECAUSE OF 'LEAKAGE' EFFECTS, IN BRITAIN IT WON'T BE A FACTOR OF MORE THAN **2 OR 3**, EVEN IF THE M.P.C. IS **0.8 OR 0.9**.

Keynes owed a great debt for the development of the Multiplier theory to his "favourite pupil", **Richard Kahn**.

Which countries first tried Keynesian economics?

It is generally accepted that 3 major economies tried Keynesian solutions in the 1930s.
Sweden, Germany and the **US** were influenced by economists moving along the same road as Keynes.

In 1932, **Sweden** returned a Labour government committed to a programme of public investment. Sweden had not suffered in the depression as much as some other countries. Industrial production in 1932 was 89% of its 1929 level, compared with 84% in Britain, 72% in France and 53% in Germany and the US.

LEVELS
OF
INDUSTRIAL
OUTPUT
IN
1932

1929 LEVEL

SWEDEN   BRITAIN   FRANCE   GERMANY   U.S.A.

.......but unemployment had still increased sharply.

However, recovery was swift. By 1934, real output had regained its 1929 level and by 1935 was 7% above it. Growth continued in the second half of the 1930s and the finance minister was happy to increase the budget deficit to stimulate the economy. He was influenced by a group of economists, particularly Gunnar Myrdal, who had been thinking along Keynesian lines for a number of years.

The German Example

Germany also achieved dramatic growth from its low point of 1932.
In that year, industrial production was more than 40% below its 1929 level and there were 6 million people unemployed. By 1938, industrial production was 25% above the 1929 level and unemployment had been virtually eliminated.

Was Adolf Hitler aware of Keynes?

Keynes certainly did not approve of Hitler's authoritarian methods.

Nevertheless, one of the Nazis' political ambitions - the abolition of mass unemployment - accorded exactly with that of Keynes. Hitler did not have to worry about the Reichsbank whining about balanced budgets.

Final Solution not Keynesian Solutions

On May 1st, 1933, Hitler announced his 4-Year Plan for abolishing unemployment. On the demand side there was the Reinhardt Programme of public works. This was financed, not by borrowing (in 1933, no-one would lend money - even to the government)..

On the supply side, unemployment was attacked by a whole series of measures, including a vigorous campaign against the employment of women.

The state and party bureaucracy absorbed many workers as did, after 1935, the armed forces.

The schemes were spectacularly effective. Unemployment fell by 3 million in 2 years, while industrial production rose by 30%.

A Keynesian Parody

In a democratic country, the financing of this recovery - effectively by the printing of money - would have been inflationary.

Germany's recovery from depression was classically Keynesian. It was, however, only possible because the Nazis' political ambitions overrode any objections to the long term effects of the stimulus.
The state was not seen as the guardian of a liberated economic life.
Economic life was seen as a servant of the state.

The economic aim of Nazism was **mobilization for war!**

Prophetic Words, Again!

Keynes foresaw where the Nazi approach might lead........

Rescuing the United States

By the time **Franklin D.Roosevelt (1882-1945)** replaced **Herbert Hoover (1874-1964)** as President in the winter of 1932/3, the economic situation was catastrophic.

The national income was less than half what it had been four short years before. Nearly 13 million Americans - about one quarter of the labour force - were desperately seeking jobs. The machinery for sheltering and feeding the unemployed was breaking down everywhere under a growing burden. On the morning of Roosevelt's inauguration, every bank in America had locked its doors. It was now a matter of seeing whether a representative democracy could conquer economic collapse. It was a matter of staving off violence - even, some thought , - *revolution*.

– Arthur Schlesinger

Even Keynes was bemused by the size of the problem. He wrote to Lydia:

....Even I would hardly think that I could know what to do if I were President, though I expect I should when it came to it.......

I RESPONDED WITH A BARRAGE OF MEASURES IN MY FIRST "HUNDRED DAYS."

Franklin D. Roosevelt

Although many of these measures would certainly now be seen as Keynesian, FDR himself did not regard them as part of a coherent "Keynesian" plan. He saw them as ways of relieving distress until more normal times returned.

A hotch-potch of recovery measures

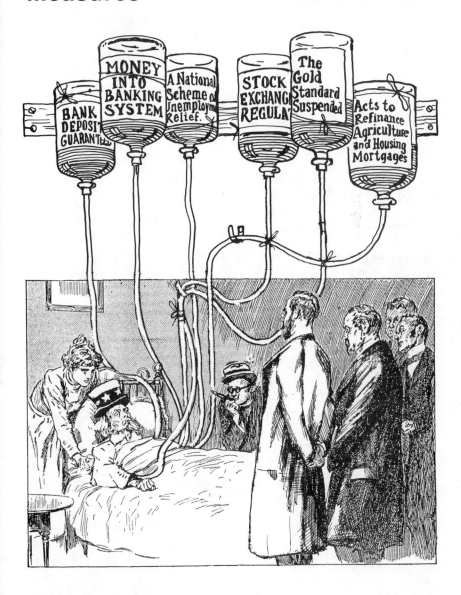

America's first experiment in state socialism was tried in the form of the Tennessee Valley Authority. There were organized, if slightly contradictory, efforts to raise both prices and wages.

On fiscal policy, Roosevelt showed his adherence to the classical balanced budget concepts by offsetting a $3.3 billion public works programme with other economies elsewhere in public spending.

And it seemed to work. There was an immediate revival in confidence. Industrial production almost doubled between March and July 1933. Keynes was sceptical as to whether the recovery would last.

ONE FEARS THE PRESIDENT IS DEPENDING FAR TOO MUCH ON PSYCHOLOGICAL AS DISTINCT FROM REAL FACTORS. THE OPERATION OF THE PSYCHOLOGICAL FACTORS IS BEING FLATTERED BY THE FACT THAT IT BEGAN AT A POINT WHEN THE USA WAS ENTITLED TO A STRONG UPWARD REACTION, EVEN WITHOUT ADVENTITIOUS AIDS. ON THE OTHER HAND, REAL FACTORS, SUCH AS OPEN-MARKET OPERATIONS AND PUBLIC WORKS, ARE BEING TACKLED MUCH TOO TIMIDLY.

THUS IT IS NOT IMPOSSIBLE THAT THE PROGRAMME MAY CARRY THROUGH SUCCESSFULLY.

Keynes was hopeful that the **Multiplier** effect would be strong.

War is one solution....

Whatever else it did, the **Second World War (1939-45)** solved the unemployment problem in all industrial countries. It also brought a massive increase in output.

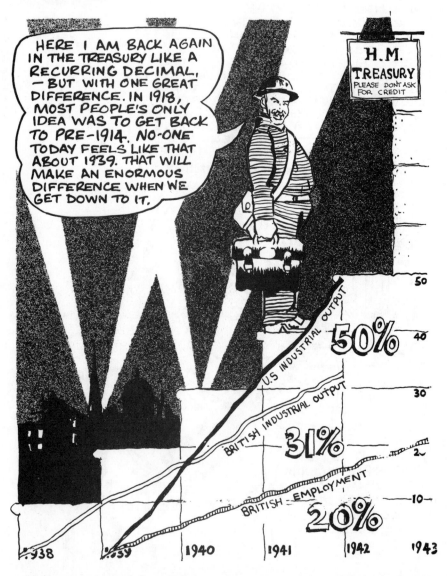

It made people determined that full employment, by whatever means, should be preserved once the war was over.

From the Cradle to the Grave

This mood was reinforced by the publication of the Beveridge Report in 1942 **(Sir William Beveridge, 1879 - 1963)**, describing itself as a plan to provide social security for all from cradle to grave. There was a general fear, rooted in the experience of the slump that followed the First World War, that mass unemployment would return again.........

UNLESS GOVERNMENTS PURSUE ITS PREVENTION AS THEIR TOP PRIORITY

There was a general feeling throughout Europe that the Establishment of the1930s had failed and that a fresh start must be made.

IF THE STATE CAN EFFECTIVELY MOBILIZE FOR WAR....

....IT SHOULD NOW BE ABLE TO CREATE A BETTER PEACE.

Paying for the War

Keynes' small book *How to Pay for the War* was already looking ahead. Whereas his *General Theory* had attempted to solve the problem of **deficient** demand, *How to Pay for the War* addressed the new problem of **excess** demand.

By the end of the War, Keynesian ideas were fully accepted at the Treasury. Already in 1944, the Government had published a White Paper on Employment policy....

Keynes' ideas were also accepted in the U.S. as a preventative to the horrors of the 1920s. Keynesian economics, seen essentially as a means of providing the elusive goal of full employment, had established itself as the new orthodoxy. Keynes had conquered both the academic and political worlds, not only as a solution to depressions, but for a general economic stabilization policy.

Keynesianism in War-time and After.

From the War onwards, the British Government pursued what it perceived to be Keynesian policies. The Economic section of the War Cabinet secretariat included such notable Keynesians as **James Meade** and **Richard Stone** who were extremely influencial, as was Keynes himself, over Kingsley Wood's 1941 Budget and the 1944 White Paper on employment policy.

For the remainder of the 1940s and on into the 1950s and 1960s, successive Labour and Conservative governments employed a variety of fiscal and monetary measures designed to maintain full employment without, it was hoped, causing too much inflation or damage to the balance of payments.

In the USA, Keynes' ideas were influential on government and the public's attitude to the role of government. The Employment Act of 1946 and later the Humphrey-Hawkins Act, gave the government responsibility for employment and prices.

Keynes' influence on British government policy during and immediately after the Second World War was profound. He was adroit at exploiting his personal contacts at the highest level and was personally involved in most aspects of war-time high policy both at home and in the USA.

The Bretton Woods Agreement, 27 July 1944.

The Bretton Woods conference was convened as a result of planning in both the U.S.A. and Britain by teams under Keynes in Britain and the under-secretary of the U.S. Treasury, Harry Dexter White, in the U.S. Both wanted to design a liberal economic order to avoid the harmful policies of the 1920s and 1930s when commercial warfare and competitive devaluations had brought depression and mass unemployment.

Seen here enjoying a joke at the Bretton Woods Conference, New Hampshire, last Friday are top economic experts **Harry D. White** (*left*) and **John Maynard Keynes**.

The principles behind the Bretton Woods conference were:

1. international monetary co-operation through international agencies with defined functions and powers

2. high sustained levels of international investment through the creation of of an international investment bank

3. a system of unhindered trade and convertible currencies

4. the support of gold and currency reserves to prevent short-run balance of payments deficits leading to policies with undesirable effects of unemployment

5. the balancing of payments *disequilibria* is the responsibility of both the surplus and deficit country.

International investment was to be carried out through the **International Monetary Fund** which was designed:

1. to promote international monetary co-operation through a permanent institution,

2. to facilitate the expansion of world trade and to maintain high levels of employment,

3. to promote exchange stability and to give confidence to members by making the Fund's resources available to them under adequate safeguards to correct maladjustments in their balance of payments.

The Fund came into operation on 27th December 1945 when it had 30 members. Initially its work was somewhat eclipsed by that of the **International Bank for Reconstruction and Development (World Bank)**, whose task in rehabilitating Europe and lending funds to the undeveloped nations seemed more pressing. Also in the 1940s and 1950s the liberal policies, so important to the IMF, were difficult in a world governed by exchange controls, tariffs and quotas. In 1958, the return of most European currencies to convertibility with the $ brought the IMF to the fore.

Britain's "Financial Dunkirk"

Keynes, more than anyone, appreciated Britain's precarious financial position. He warned the government that the country faced the dire prospect of a "financial Dunkirk".

Keynes was despatched by the newly elected Labour Government to negotiate a $6 billion loan from the Americans.

Furthermore, the Bretton Woods Agreement meant sterling would be freely convertible within a year and that the imperial preferences would be abandoned. Finally Britain would have to settle with her sterling creditors by 1951.

"Was the USA really ungenerous?"

The British were not the only ones clamouring for American aid. As Keynes told the House of Lords in the autumn of 1945....

"Capitalism internationally safeguarded".

Keynes pointed out that the terms negotiated were more generous than those achieved by other European countries.Furthermore they were a step along the road he had been advocating since 1920.

There was a reluctance to accept the terms. The Economist said...

Keynes Dies...

These negotiations exhausted Keynes, who had suffered a serious heart attack as early as 1937. On 20 April 1946, he died at his Sussex farmhouse, Tilton, in the arms of his beloved Lydia. His ashes were scattered on the Downs above Tilton.

Keynes' will had requested that his ashes be deposited in the crypt of King's College, Cambridge, but his brother Geoffrey proved to be a less than conscientious executor.

Geoffrey's son, Richard, faced a dilemma when Lydia died 35 years later, as the will requested her ashes be put beside her husband's at King's.

"We've never had it so good".

Did Keynesianism work? It seemed to. For at least 25 years after the war the advanced capitalist world boomed as never before. Unemployment was lower than at any time in the previous 100 years.

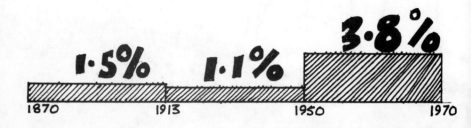

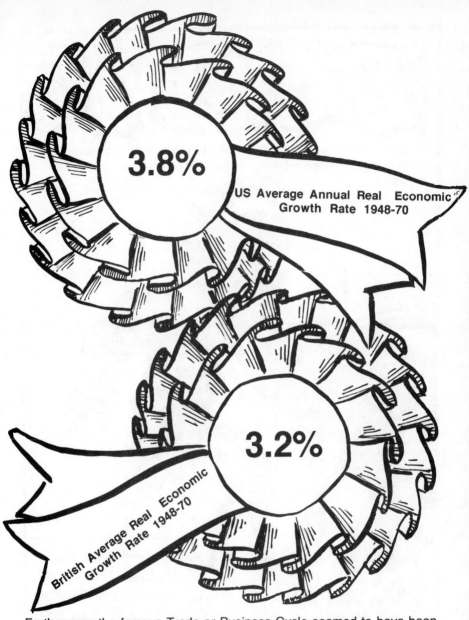

3.8%

US Average Annual Real Economic Growth Rate 1948-70

3.2%

British Average Real Economic Growth Rate 1948-70

Furthermore the famous Trade or Business Cycle seemed to have been tamed by Keynesian demand management. There were ups and downs in activity and levels of unemployment, but these were mild and even the downturns seemed no more than "growth recessions" constituting no more than a slowdown in the rate of growth. In 1969 Martin Brofenbrenner published a well-researched document called *"Is the Business Cycle Obsolete?"*

BOOM! №1

There have been arguments over how actively Keynesian governments were responsible for this boom, and other factors were put forward to explain it.

THE LONG POLITICAL SOLIDARITY OF THE ADVANCED CAPITALIST COUNTRIES, ALL OF WHOM FELT THREATENED BY EITHER COMMUNIST RUSSIA OR CHINA.

THE BACKLOG OF TECHNOLOGICAL INNOVATIONS WAITING TO BE EXPLOITED...

THE DEPRESSED ASPIRATIONS OF THE WORKERS, WHICH BROUGHT ABOVE-AVERAGE PERFORMANCE WITHOUT EXCESSIVE PAY DEMANDS...

THE GROWING LIBERALIZATION OF TRADE UNDER GATT.

GATT, the General Agreements on Tariffs and Trade, was established in Geneva in 1947 and became operational on 1st January 1948. It's main role has been to conduct a series of tariff negotiations working on two principles from its Articles of Agreement.

1. Trade should be conducted on the basis of non-discrimination between countries.

2. Existing preferential arrangements should be gradually reduced through negotiation until they are finally eliminated.

Although GATT was hampered by its lack of powers to compel nations to dismantle controls, over the following 40 years it was successful in gradually reducing restrictions on international trade.

The "Fine-Tuning" of Keynesianism.

Indeed, Keynes himself never advocated the "fine-tuning" tactics employed by successive British governments, but rather the strategic "socialization of investment" whereby action should be taken to encourage investment in both the public and private sectors.

Nevertheless governments pursued active Keynesian policies and recognized the need to take expansionary fiscal action when faced with the collapse of demand. In Britain Keynesian policies were pursued continuously untill the mid 1970s.

Fine-Tuning Demand.

On a number of occasions in the early and late 1950s, early 60s and early 70s, demand fell below the productive potential. The government responded with a combination of measures to increase effective demand.

Fiscal Policies.
-increases in government expenditure
-reductions in taxes

INFLATIONARY!

Monetary Policies
-reductions in interest rates
-relaxation of controls on bank advances and hire purchase.

MORE CREDIT!

Phillips Curve

In the late 1950s, A.W. Phillips studied Britain's economy for the previous 100 years and noted that there had been an inverse relationship between the level of unemployment and the rate of increase of money wages. When unemployment was high, wages increased slowly but when it was low, they increased a good deal faster. Common sense would suggest the reasons.

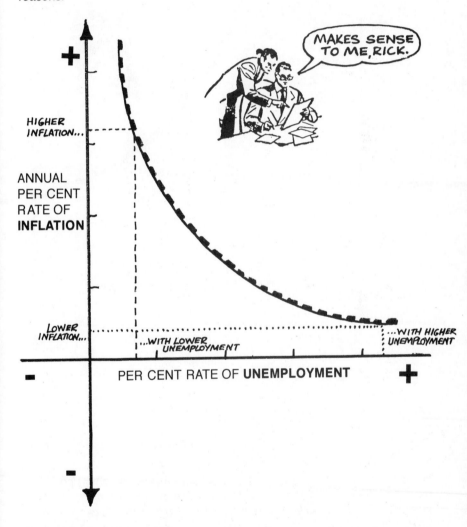

It was suggested that people would have to settle for a trade-off between levels of inflation and unemployment.

"What happens when unemployment and inflation BOTH increase?"

In the late 1960s and 70s the Phillips Curve moved up **and** to the right as both unemployment and inflation rose together.

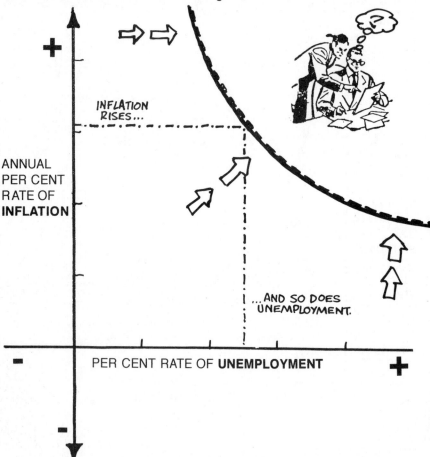

By the middle of the 1970s, people were fed up with both Keynes and Phillips, who no longer seemed able to provide a cure for either unemployment or inflation. Critics of Keynes had always pointed to the dangers inherent in budget deficits, most notably inflation, but for the 25 years after the War, inflation scarcely posed any threat. In the USA it averaged 2.5% and in Britain 4.1%. This was high by earlier standards, but not by those of the 1970s.

Meanwhile, in the USA.....

Jack Kennedy's administration was full of committed Keynesians determined to achieve full employment.

Eisenhower before him had been more interested in eliminating inflationary tendencies through fiscal expansion.

I'M CONCENTRATING ON THE PRE-KEYNESIAN TENDENCY OF TRYING TO BALANCE THE FEDERAL BUDGET.

RESULT? UNEMPLOYMENT ROSE IN THE 50s AND REACHED 7% BY 1960!

Increased federal expenditure followed by tax cuts brought an 8-year boom. At the end of the 1960s the newly appointed President Nixon said.......

WE ARE ALL KEYNESIANS NOW!

Rejection of Keynes in the 1970s

The collapse of the Bretton Woods system in the early 1970s and the explosive rise in the price of commodities, especially oil, brought to an end the steady, low-inflation growth the industrialized world had enjoyed since 1945.

Keynesian policies did not seem to work any more and a new *ism* came into fashion - **Monetarism**.

What is Monetarism?

The monetarist rejected the post- war Keynesian orthodoxy.

Governments should **NOT** interfere to manipulate the level of demand.

A little inflation is **NOT** acceptable to maintain full employment.

The "New" Classical Economists

The monetarists, led by their main publicist, Milton Friedman (b.1912), seemed to be going back to the 19th century classical economists of whom Keynes had been so critical.

The Natural Rate of Unemployment

Monetarists criticized attempts by Keynes-inspired goverments to keep unemployment at below the so-called "natural rate".

If this inflation rate was regarded as too high because of past mistakes then the money supply would have to be reduced in order to lower the rate of inflation, even if, in the short term, this meant *higher* unemployment.

"And what about HIGH unemployment?"

If this left unemployment high, the answer was not to try and reduce unemployment below its natural rate, but to reduce the natural rate itself. This would have to be done not by macro-economic measures but by micro-economic or what became known as "supplyside" measures.

In the monetarists view, trade unions had grown too powerful and inflexible. (Keynes wasn't a great fan of unions either.) In the 60s and 70s, union inflexibility was held to blame for **unemployment and inflation rising together.**

141

The "Selsdon Man" Monetarist

Prime Minister Edward Heath (for a time nicknamed "Selsdon Man", following a Tory front-bench conference at the Selsdon Park Hotel from which tough "monetarist" pronouncements emerged), began to flirt with monetarist policies from 1970. He shrank back as unemployment breached the **1 million** mark in early 1972.

Even the Labour government of the late 1970s was forced to adopt what some considered to be anti-Keynesian policies following the financial crisis of 1976. Prime Minister Callaghan told the disbelieving delegates at the 1976 Labour Party Conference.....

Now, for Selsdon Woman!

It was Prime Minister Margaret Thatcher who embraced the monetarist policy of reducing the money supply and trying to improve the supply-side of the economy.

The main target of the monetarists and Mrs Thatcher were the unions, who, she said, had long been abusing their monopoly power to keep wages above the market clearing rate.

The closed-shop union strategy had prevented those who were prepared to work for the "market" rate from doing so.

If real wages fell, more would be employed. A fall in the natural rate of unemployment was the monetarists' main aim.

Monetarist Remedies for Unemployment

The stance of monetary policy should be judged by the behaviour of the money supply rather than that of interest rates. Inflation, leading to unemployment, is caused by an excess of money. Therefore, to reduce inflation and ultimately unemployment, the supply of money must be cut back.

Monetary policy is the **control of credit** both in terms of supply and interest rates, whereas fiscal policy is essentially **taxation**. Monetary policy, rather than fiscal policy, should be used as the more powerful instrument of stabilization policy.

The time-lags of policy measures are long and unsure in their effects on natural fluctuations in the private sector. Governments would do better to refrain from attempts at stabilization and concentrate on preventing monetary policy from becoming a destabilizing factor by fixing a target rate of growth of the money stock, irrespective of the state of effective demand.

Monetary policy can destabilize if the money supply is either too excessive or too restrictive, or if interest rates are too high or too low. If the state of effective demand is already high, releasing more money into the system or reducing interest rates (or both, as Chancellor of the Exchequer Nigel Lawson did in 1988) can lead to excess demand and increased inflation.

Friedman's views sparked off a strong academic debate and were taken up by the political right as a means of attacking state expenditure and intervention with its consequent effects of stoking up inflation.
The monetarists' timing was propitious.

Stagflation.

Milton Friedman had been working hard for almost a generation to establish the intellectual justification for his monetarist views. The stagflation (no growth combined with high inflation) of the 1970s provided the perfect backdrop for practical politicians to adopt his views, so eloquently propounded in his *Free to Choose*.

Did Monetarism Work?

In Britain, Keynesian demand management was completely abandoned. The budget deficit was reduced and the growth of money supply was slowed down.

What about the "side effects" of monetarist policy?

Milton Friedman, in support of Thatcher, said to the House of Commons Treasury and Civil Service Comittee in June 1980...

The Failure of Monetarism

Inflation did fall, though some would argue it had nothing to do with the money supply and everything to do with rising unemployment.

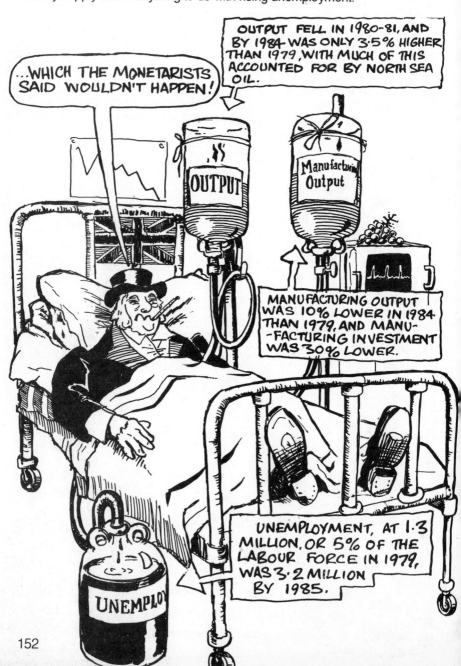

And Reaganomics?

Were things better in the USA, where President Reagan also said he was pursuing monetarist policies?
Yes.

So monetarism worked in the U.S.A.?
No.
Because whatever Reagan said or thought he was doing, he was in fact pursuing not monetarist, but **Keynesian**, policies.

The budget deficit rose from 60 billion, or 2% of Gross Domestic Product in 1980, to 200 billion or 5% of G.D.P. in 1985.

Was it fair to blame Keynesian policies for the stagflation of the 1970s?

One of the main causes of the world-wide inflation of the 1970s was the Vietnam War and the refusal of the U.S. Government to pay for it by raising taxes. Keynes would certainly have argued for raising taxes. His pamphlet, *How to Pay for the War*, had shown how increased government expenditure in war-time was inflationary.

President Johnson ignored his Keynesian advisers until 1968, by which time the "inflation horse was out of the barn".

The Contradictions of Keynes.

It could be argued that Keynesianism was blamed for a phenomenon that would never have happened, were he still alive to control events.

In analyzing Keynes, it is difficult to tie him down as he contradicted himself on certain key issues. For example, at one moment he was a strong advocate of Free Trade, saying that to argue that trade barriers reduce unemployment...

...INVOLVES THE PROTECTIONIST FALLACY IN ITS GROSSEST AND CRUDEST FORM... I BELIEVE IN FREE TRADE BECAUSE... IT IS THE ONLY POLICY WHICH IS TECHNICALLY SOUND AND INTELLECTUALLY RIGHT.

Later he spoke in favour of protection.

Was he for the working-class or contemptuous? On the General Strike he said ..

Nor was he keen on trade unions.

ONCE THE OPPRESSED, NOW THE TYRANTS, WHOSE SELFISH AND SECTIONAL PRETENSIONS NEED TO BE BRAVELY OPPOSED.

He was not a great respecter of businessmen, feeling they were lazy and stupid. He saw a three-generation cycle.

He felt that Britain in the 1920s and 1930s was full of third-generation businessmen. He was to say in 1945...

IF BY SOME SAD GEOGRAPHICAL SLIP THE AMERICAN AIR FORCE (IT IS TOO LATE NOW TO HOPE FOR MUCH FROM THE ENEMY) WERE TO DESTROY EVERY FACTORY ON THE NORTH EAST COAST AND IN LANCASHIRE (AT AN HOUR WHEN DIRECTORS WERE SITTING THERE AND NO ONE ELSE), WE SHOULD HAVE NOTHING TO FEAR. HOW ELSE WE ARE TO REGAIN THE EXUBERANT INEXPERIENCE WHICH IS NECESSARY, IT SEEMS, FOR SUCCESS, I CANNOT SURMISE.

On the other hand, he was very friendly with the businessman **Samuel Courtauld (1876-1947)**. Keynes appreciated the need to encourage business investment to bring growth and reduce unemployment.

And businesses must have the expectation of profit.

"Such expectations partly depend on non-monetary influence, on peace and war, inventions, laws, race, education, population and so forth. But their power to put their projects into execution on terms which they deem attractive almost entirely depends on the behaviour of the banking and monetary system".

Myths about Keynes

There are also myths that have grown up about Keynes.
The first is that he was tolerant of inflation.
This was not so.
He opposed it throughout his life.

MODERN INDIVIDUALISTIC SOCIETY, ORGANIZED ON THE LINES OF CAPITALISTIC INDUSTRY, CANNOT SUPPORT A VIOLENTLY FLUCTUATING STANDARD OF VALUE, WHETHER THE MOVEMENT IS UPWARDS OR DOWNWARDS. ITS ARRANGEMENTS PRESUME AND ABSOLUTELY REQUIRE A REASONABLY STABLE STANDARD. UNLESS WE GIVE IT SUCH A STANDARD, THIS SOCIETY WILL BE STRICKEN WITH A MORTAL DISEASE AND WILL NOT SURVIVE. ONLY BY WISELY REGULATING THE CREATION OF CURRENCY AND CREDIT ALONG NEW LINES CAN WE PROTECT SOCIETY AGAINST THE ATTACKS AND CRITICISMS OF SOCIALIST AND COMMUNIST INNOVATORS.

The second is that he was an advocate of what became known as "fine-tuning", i.e. short-term tinkering with fiscal policy to try and iron out fluctuations in the business cycle. British governments since the war have constantly indulged in such fine-tuning. One of the favourites, especially in the 1960s and 1970s, was the change of credit restrictions on the purchase of consumer durables. Keynes was not in favour of such short- term activities.

Keynes, the Gold Standard and the ERM

There is an interesting and important Keynesian lesson to be drawn from comparing the Gold Standard of the 1920s and 30s with the attempt in the late 80s to create a stable **Exchange Rate Mechanism** for European currencies.

Both the Gold Standard and the ERM were attempts to impose a stable currency discipline on the economy by ensuring that international competition would force manufacturers to keep their costs down - in both cases by **shedding labour**. Given time - unfortunately a long time, many years, even decades - the strategy might have worked and we might have finished up with low-cost, efficient industry. In modern democracies, people will not tolerate the sacrifices involved.

166

What was behind the City speculators' rush against the pound on Black Wednesday, 16th September 1992? The exchange rate of the Pound, like other major currencies, was pegged to the strong German Deutschmark backed by high interest rates. When the US cut its interest rates in an attempt to end recession, the Dollar inevitably went into sharp fall, putting strain on all the major European currencies in the ERM. Interest rates were also high in the U.K. (15% in 1989) and recession threatened to deepen into a slump.

Prime Minister John Major was under the illusion that the British people were prepared to endure many years of deep recession to secure a magical goal of **zero inflation**. He believed this might be achieved if the Pound remained tied to an overvalued rate against the Deutschmark.

IT IS MY FIRM BELIEF THAT THE POUND WILL REPLACE THE DEUTSCHMARK AS THE BENCHMARK CURRENCY OF EUROPE.

AND WE IN THE BUNDESBANK KNOW THAT A REALIGNMENT OF CURRENCIES WITHIN THE E.R.M. IS NECESSARY.

"REALIGNMENT"? DOESN'T HE MEAN **DEVALUATION?**

The Pound fell steeply, it came off the ERM and interest rates were immediately slashed.

fusal to cut interest rates angers France, forces banks to spend billions pro

Bundesbank torpe

Decision not to cut key discount rate shows wish to protect German ma

Bundesbank puts EMS in je

JOHN EISENHAMMER

risis at the he

Speculators

at had been widely

Euro crisis

Nick Goodway

CHANCE

off cutting rates for a few weeks
but that the arguments are now

points to 4% UK

restructured this weekend, sterling is bound to rise,' he says.

rates are cut we run the risk
sucking in imports which mea
that there is a very real risk

Currency

dogma that

He expressed
rate cut would
S".

e annual infla-
accelerating to
han twice the
im-term goal,
supply figures

Strain placed on alliance as
franc comes under pressure

THE BUNDESBANK's decision not

cost the

JULIAN NUNDY

come from worse-than-expected sta
tistics since the beginning of this year

French dear

up franc and threatens monetary union

oes ERM

pardy

rt of Europe

The European Exchange Rate Mechanism cou
break up this weekend.

and governments o

ermany issu

RM ultimatu

LOOKS LIKE I'M DUE FOR A **COMEBACK**...

...working. Now that would
be good for Europe.'

es

ending money was worth
other £50,' he added.

expec
Th
wor
atio
co
nt
e N
Tj

Where is the Keynesian revolution now?

It had looked as though the Keynesians were banished for ever, but the world recession of the early 1990s led to severe questioning of the Monetarist approach, which came to be seen as crude and simplistic. Keynes knew that economies and people's behaviour within them were complicated and could not be explained in such dogmatic terms. What drives a capitalist economy forward is the decision to invest and, while this investment will usually only happen in a stable environment, which governments should strive to create, the final decision comes from individual entrepreneurs and their willingness to take risks, spurred on by what Keynes called their "animal spirits".

Keynes is as relevant today as he was in the 1930s.

Publications of John Maynard Keynes

Indian Currency and Finance

Economic Consequences of the Peace

A Tract on Monetary Reform

A Treatise on Money - The Pure Theory of Money

A Treatise on Money - The Applied Theory of Money

The General Theory of Employment, Interest and Money

A Treatise on Probability

Bibliography

Keynes, Beveridge and Beyond **Tony Cutter, Karen Williams and John Williams** (Routledge and Kegan Paul, 1986)

The Making of Keynes' General Theory **Richard F. Kahn** (Cambridge University Press, 1984)

J. M. Keynes in Retrospect **Ed. Derek Crabtree and A. P. Thirlwall** (Macmillan, 1980)

Macroeconomics after Thatcher and Reagan **John N. Smithin** (Edward Egar, 1990)

The Cambridge Apostles; The Early Years **Peter Allen** (Cambridge University Press, 1978)

The Life of John Maynard Keynes **R.F. Harrod** (Macmillan, 1951)

Maynard Keynes - An Economist's Biography **D.E. Moggridge** (Routledge,1992)

Keynes' Monetary Thought **D Patinkin** (Duke University Press, 1976)

Bloomsbury Portraits **Richard Shone** (Phaidon, 1976)

John Maynard Keynes Vol.1, Hopes Betrayed 1883-1920 **Robert Skidelsky** (Viking, 1985)

John Maynard Keynes Vol.2, The Economist as Saviour 1921-37 **Robert Skidelsky** (Macmillan, 1992)

Never Again, Britain 1945-51 **Peter Hennessey** (Jonathan Cape, 1992)

The People's Peace, British History 1945-1989 **Kenneth O. Morgan** (Oxford University Press, 1990)

One of Us **Hugo Young** (Macmillan, 1989)

Post-War Britain **Alan Sked and Chris Cook** (Penguin, 1979)

The State We're In **Will Hutton** (Jonathan Cape, 1995)

John Maynard Keynes ed. **Soumitra Sharma** (Edward Elgar, 1998)

The Keynesian Revolution **Essays of Robert Eisner** (Edward Elgar, 1998)

Keynesianism and the Keynesian Revolution in America ed. **O.F. Hamouda** and **B.B. Price** (Edward Elgar, 1998)

From Boom to Bust **David Smith** (Penguin, 1992)

The Chancellors **Roy Jenkins** (Macmillan, 1998)

Margaret Thatcher, the Downing Street Years **Margaret Thatcher** (HarperCollins, 1993)

The Keynesian Revolution and its Economic Consequences **Peter Clarke** (Edward Elgar, 1998)

Acknowledgements

Artwork Assistants
Glenn Ward
Sarah Garratt

Picture Research
Helen James
Deborah Wood
Maureen Mortlock

174

Index